T0156751

ANIMAL TOTEM GUIDES: MESSAGES FOR THE WORLD

Communicating with Your Power Animal Guides

FRANKI STORLIE

iUniverse, Inc.
Bloomington

Animal Totem Guides: Messages for the World
Communicating with Your Power Animal Guides

Copyright © 2011 Franki Storlie

iUniverse books may be ordered through booksellers or by contacting:

iUniverse
1663 Liberty Drive
Bloomington, IN 47403
www.iuniverse.com
1-800-Authors (1-800-288-4677)

ISBN: 978-1-4620-2069-0 (sc)
ISBN: 978-1-4620-2071-3 (hc)
ISBN: 978-1-4620-2070-6 (e)

Printed in the United States of America

iUniverse rev. date: 5/27/2011

Contents

Part Two: Personal Growth

Part Three: Resources and References

A Message from Franki

Dear Reader,

I want to personally thank you for reading my book and allowing me to share my teachings, stories, and experiences with you.

I believe that every person has a spirit heart and soul waiting to be reawakened and longing to seek spiritual knowledge. Every person has a desire to connect with his or her own soul and spiritual guides, including power animal totem guides. It is my intent with this book, which focuses on our partners, the animals, to connect readers to their power animal guides and, above all, to connect readers to their spirit heart and soul. It is my heart's desire that readers will also recognize and appreciate the earth, the elements, the trees, and above all, the animals.

I am called a teacher, a healer, a drummer, a shaman, and a friend to everyone I meet (and a friend to all the animals and earth as well). While titles like this are wonderful, my dream, vision, and intent is to assist every person in finding his or her own unique and special spiritual pathway so that he or she can truly find joy, peace, wisdom, and love in his or her life. For you see, I know and believe with all my heart that all people are very special, and I believe that every word and thought they wish to share with me is important.

Ever since I was a young child, I have loved animals of all types. My father was an accomplished horseman and well known for this skill. He was extremely talented in the breaking and training of horses. He could catch the wildest mustang on the reservation and have that horse following him around within a short period of time. He taught me to respect and honor not only horses, but all animals. As a child growing up on a ranch with three wonderful and adventuresome older sisters, I enjoyed the company of dogs, cats, horses, sheep, pigs, chickens, and cattle. I assisted my sisters, mother, and father on horseback with the cattle drives. When I was sixteen, my father bought a huge ranch of 1,500-plus acres, and this ranch is plentiful with deer, elk, an occasional cougar and bear, and many other types of wildlife. The ranch is designated by the Audubon Society as an "important bird area." I take care of this ranch with my sisters, son, and husband. So as you can see, a great portion of my life has been blessed with the opportunities to observe and communicate with the animal kingdom.

I have been studying and practicing spiritual teachings for the past twenty years. I specialize in practices of the sacred medicine wheel (not just inclusive of Native American, but a broader span of teachings) and partnering with nature to create safe and sacred space so that people can learn to meditate, connect to their inner self, and find balance in a very busy, and often chaotic, world.

I also teach a wide array of spiritual classes and offer other services. Please see my complete listing of classes and services offered in the closing chapter of this book.

Introduction

It was the vision of an eagle that first captured my unconscious. As the years flew by and the visions soared, I was inspired to capture them on paper to share with all of you. One of my power animal guides, the eagle, was always present in my spiritual journeys and meditations and said to me, "Share this vision with the people of the earth so that they will seek out the animals and become their partners in order to heal themselves and save the earth!"

My Vision for Earth and All of Humanity

I have a vision that has been shown to me for the past several years and recurs periodically during my shamanic journeys. When this happens in my journeys, I connect with medicine women and men (shamans) of all cultures and spiritual beliefs on every continent on earth. I can clearly see their faces and, sometimes, exactly what they are wearing and the expressions on their faces. I connect to the African shamans, the aborigine shamans, the European shamans, the Celtic shamans, the South American shamans, the North American shamans, the Tibetan shamans, the Native American shamans, and so forth throughout all the continents on Mother Earth. I then see all kinds of medicine wheels, representing all of these cultures and spiritual beliefs, connecting and spinning, until finally, they all connect and become one golden sacred medicine wheel (the sacred hoop). This sacred hoop connects Mother Earth and all of creation on the earth to the Mother/Father Creator.

The eagles, from all the directions, meet at the center of this golden sacred medicine wheel and sit in council with all of the animals on Mother Earth. They decide to speak, and they say that it is now time for all of the humans on earth to come together in oneness, to dissolve disagreements, wars, duality, hate, fear, and injustices. They say that it is time to be tolerant, patient, compassionate, truthful, and respectful of all beliefs and cultures.

All of the sacred teachings of all cultures and beliefs from every continent on earth come together in oneness and acknowledgment of each other in a sacred and respectful manner at the center of this golden sacred medicine wheel. Mother Earth and all of creation are then immersed in divine love energy, and the earth, all of humanity, and all creation on the earth are instantly healed and brought into the light of oneness with Mother/Father Creator.

I asked, during each journey, why I was being shown this and what I was to do. The answer was always clear: I am to share my spiritual experiences and teachings that I have acquired over the past twenty years through my spiritual teachers and guides, power animal guides, shamanic journeys, and personal experiences.

So, it is with great humility, love, and respect that I offer my experiences and teachings to you in this book.

PART ONE:

Animal Totem Stories and Meditations

CHAPTER 1:
The Power Animals as Our Partners

It is my belief that each person on this earth is not only special but spiritual. Each person has a spiritual soul that is connected to God (Mother/Father Creator), Mother Earth, and all of creation on the earth. For you see, everything and everyone is related and connected. All of creation includes the humans, the animals, the earth, the environment, the plants, the trees, the mountains, the elements, the rocks, and so forth. Through your spiritual soul and heart, you can become a partner with your power animal guides and Mother Earth and assist in healing the earth and, more importantly, in healing yourself.

Every person has at least nine power animal totem guides that surround his or her body and spirit: east, south, west, north, upper, lower, within, right side, and left side. They walk beside you to protect, guide, teach, and communicate wisdom to you through your soul and heart. They are like guardian angels, from either the domestic or wild animal kingdoms, and include birds, fish, reptiles, and insects.

- Your east power animal guide assists you with your spiritual growth and leads you on your path to illumination.
- Your south power animal guide protects your pathway and assists you with physical healing.
- Your west power animal guide assists you with searching deep within through meditation to find inner answers and truth. It assists you with balancing your emotions and being true to yourself.
- Your north power animal guide teaches you wisdom and the importance of being silent, being balanced and sharp mentally, and knowing when to speak and when to listen.
- Your upper power animal guide gives you access to the upper dimensions and realms of the upper world and assists with connecting you to your guides, angels, and Mother/Father Creator.
- Your lower power animal guide connects you directly with Mother Earth and the other inner and lower world dimensions and realms. This totem keeps you grounded to Mother Earth.
- Your within power animal guide is usually your guardian power animal guide from birth. It guides you to find your true spiritual pathway, to find joy and truth in your life. It assists you with developing your intuitive abilities.
- Your right power animal guide is your male side and is your protector, your warrior spirit. He assists you with balancing your male energy.
- Your left power animal guide is your female side and is your nurturer. She assists you with balancing your female energy.

Come with me now, and I will share with you wonderful and adventuresome power animal stories. Each story will have a lesson from the power animal that is portrayed in the story. Each story will assist you with finding your own power animal(s) and to find your own sacred pathway.

Interspersed between the animal stories will be teachings that I will share with you regarding how to connect with your own power animal(s), the elements, and Mother Earth. More importantly, I will assist you with connecting with your inner self, your soul, and finding your sacred spiritual pathway with your power animal(s). By finding your spiritual pathway with your power animal(s), you will begin the process of healing yourself and the earth. You may find yourself transformed as you work through the process.

I know that each of you has special animal stories to share as well. I hope that after reading this book, each of you will reflect on them and share your special animal stories with others.

The Animals as Our Partners

When I talk about animals being our partners, I include all animals, domestic and wild, as well as insects, reptiles, fish, whales, dolphins, and so forth. An example of a wonderful animal partner is the loyalty displayed by our domestic family dogs. They protect our family members, and no matter what we do to them, they unconditionally forgive us and are loyal to the family.

If you take the time to observe your domestic pets, they can teach you a lot about survival on earth, and moreover, they can teach you how to interact with each other, for again they emulate the qualities of unconditional loyalty, forgiveness, and love.

Animals out in the wild, if you observe them, are powerful examples of survival and clear communication, both silent and verbal, and through their actions, they teach us useful interpersonal skills.

I believe that all of the animals desire us to be good stewards and guardians of the earth and the environment. If we, as humans, are ready to communicate with them and show them we truly care about them and the earth, the result could be that the earth and all of humanity will be healed.

Messages from the Power Animals

I am eagle and I wish to say, "We, the animals, are here now for all of humanity and Mother Earth. We are ready to connect with each and every person on earth and become his or her power animal guide. We can lighten hearts and communicate with each person."

I am bear and I wish to say, "We are all related: the humans, the earth, the animals, the rocks and minerals, the elements, the trees and plants, and so forth. It is time for all of us to come together and communicate in order to be good guardians of the earth."

I am coyote and I ask that "everyone respect the animal kingdom and the plant nations, for they feed us when we are hungry. Bless them and express appreciation for all that we receive from them."

I am owl and I wish to say, "The earth is shifting, and with this shift will come a great ray of light and divine love that will lift the earth and all of creation on the earth to a level of peace, love, joy, wisdom, and truth."

Chapter 2:
Coyote Medicine:
The Beginning of My Spiritual Awakening

I swerved and was startled as a large and very light colored coyote just barely brushed the side of my car for the third consecutive morning as I left for work at 7:44 a.m. Why was the coyote acting as if my car hit it, yet it was not hurt, because it would then stop in the roadway and look back at me? It would then run across the pasture as if nothing had happened! The coyote was a large male, and his coat was almost white. He seemed to be full of wisdom, and a feeling of love and warmth came over me as I watched him.

After the third morning of this same experience, I realized that this was an unusual encounter with the coyote. I loved coyotes and would always look for them on my trips to the mountains. I had read a lot about coyotes, and other animals, and how they can come into your life to offer guidance and assistance as your power animal guide or guardian angel.

When I arrived at work on the third morning after my encounter with the coyote, I tripped on a book in the hallway. I worked in the business office for the school district, and it was unusual for a book to be in the hallway. When I picked up the book, I saw that it was about coyotes. The book contained not only information about the physical habits of the coyote, but information about the spiritual significance of the coyote as well. Because I thought I did not have time to read the book, I asked my office assistant to return the book to the library, which was housed in another building of the school district.

On the fourth morning, interestingly, I did not have an encounter with the coyote and my car; however, the coyote book was on my desk when I arrived at work. I had no idea how the book ended up on my desk. I asked my office assistant if he had in fact returned the book to the library. He confirmed that he had. No one else seemed to know how or why the book was on my desk, so I decided to read it. The book was very fascinating and informative about the spiritual significance of coyotes.

That evening, I had a dream and saw the coyote in my dream. The coyote led me to where I could see a person writing down notes at a desk. The person seemed to be angry and was writing in a scheming and deceptive manner about another person. I recognized the person as someone I worked with every day. The information that was being written down was negative and could potentially be harmful to the other employee. After waking up and reflecting on the information shown to me in the dream, I shared with my supervisor that I believed there was a communication problem between the two employees. The information received in the dream was invaluable in solving a very serious problem at work.

Needless to say, this catapulted me into searching and learning more about animals and how, as our power animal totem guides, they assist us and communicate to us valuable learning experiences and information. This was an amazing occurrence to have a dream and to be able to then go to my actual job and solve a problem because of the information given to me by my power animal guide, who was talking to me in my dreamtime through the spiritual realms. This experience with coyote was the beginning of my quest to find my spiritual pathway.

Characteristics/Messages

The coyote is often called the trickster, as he/she will trick you into seeing what is truth, rather than what you want to believe. The coyote is a clever shape-shifter and can change his/her form and messages in order to show you the truth. Coyote will show you what you need to pay attention to and what is going on in your life so that you can change your pathway. Coyote can warn you about others trying to deceive or trick you, and is a protector of your pathway in life. He/she is a strong ally to have and call upon for discerning the truth about situations and people. Coyotes are able to survive in big cities right alongside humans, even though many humans try to diminish the coyote population.

Meditation with Coyote

Call upon coyote to assist you when you want your pathway cleared of deception and when you want to see the truth.

Sit facing the direction of south outside in nature or indoors. Close your eyes and visualize a pathway in front of you facing south. Through your heart chakra, feel coyote, smell coyote, stroke coyote's hair. With a drum or rattle, or even using your hands on your knee, beat a rhythm that feels like the heartbeat of coyote. See or feel coyote coming toward you and merging with you at your heart chakra center. Look into coyote's eyes. State your prayers and intentions. Sit this way as long as you wish and communicate with coyote. Be ready to see truth. Always thank coyote when you are finished.

Chapter 3:
A Message from White Elk

On my family's beautiful ranch in the mountains of Washington State, a magnificent white bull elk grazed on the ranch in the spring for several years. He was beautiful, and as I observed him, I could feel his spiritual essence, wisdom, and peacefulness. The elk was completely white, with only a few brown markings.

Because a white elk is rare, I worried that someone would shoot him for a trophy. I was troubled that this could happen, so I went on a shamanic journey to visit and connect spiritually with the white bull elk. The shamanic journey started with my drumming and feeling the heartbeat of the white elk.

As soon as I started drumming into the journey, the white elk appeared to me in my dream. He was even more magnificent in the journey, and he was in a pasture with lush grass and many colorful wildflowers of all types. He had a spiritual glow around his body. He came very close to me so that I could look into his eyes. He had tears in them and stated that he would be shot by a hunter sometime in the near future. He asked me to not grieve and to forgive the hunter. He said that he was on the earth so that people could enjoy him, even if for a short time, and to assist people in accepting animals (and people) who are different from them. He said that in the physical world, people would say he was just an albino elk, but that the spiritual people would recognize that the color white is sacred. He said that the people who are spiritually ready will connect with him and will also connect spiritually with all the elk on earth.

His message was that it is time for people of all cultures and colors to come together as a team to promote peace and healing for the entire earth and all creation on earth. He said that the elk, deer, cattle, and many other animals "go-give" to the humans by providing them with meat, fur, and other resources. The white elk stated that it is a wonderful display of appreciation to the animals when we bless our meat and food prior to eating our meals.

Characteristics/Messages

The elk represents magnificence and self-confidence! They are such wonderful communicators and family members. They promote being a close family member and openly communicating with each other. They can teach you how to be successful at teamwork. They also represent strength and endurance. They travel long distances and are able to pace themselves for endurance. They can assist you with staying on track for the long journeys in life.

Call upon elk to assist you when you want to know how to communicate well in a difficult situation for a successful outcome and you wish to acquire endurance and strength in your life. Sit facing north and imagine that you are sitting by a huge fir or pine tree in a mountain forest. Close your eyes and visualize a pathway in front of you facing north. Through your heart chakra, feel the presence of one elk or a herd of elk. See or feel elk coming toward you. Observe the elk and merge with the energy of the elk. State your prayers and intentions. Ask any questions you wish or ask for a special message of wisdom from elk. Sit this way as long as you wish and communicate with elk. Be prepared to feel strength from this journey and a different way of looking at life. Always thank elk when you are finished.

CHAPTER 4:
The Tanagers

In the spring of 2000, my sister and I were fixing range fences on our family's ranch in the Umptanum/Wenas area southwest of Ellensburg, Washington. My sister was excited about all of the songbirds in the area. She shared the names of all the types of birds that we encountered throughout the day. At one point, she suggested that I stop working in order to look more closely at the beautiful yellow and red tanagers. I said that I was more interested in the bigger birds, such as owls, hawks, and eagles; I did not go over and look at the tanagers. My sister was dismayed at my response and reiterated to me that all birds are important, not just the larger bird species.

Later that afternoon, we were taking a short break. I sat down by a mountain spring and closed my eyes for a short respite. In a few seconds, I heard a beautiful song from little songbirds close to my left ear. I slowly opened my eyes, and right by my head, sitting on the branch of the tree that I was resting against, were two gorgeous tanagers. They were so close to me that I could look into their eyes. They telepathically gave me a message. The message was that they were just as important as the bigger birds. I silently responded that I was sorry for ignoring them earlier and that I would listen to them and observe them in the future.

The tanagers sat by me on the tree branch and sang to me for about an hour. It was amazing! Even though I physically moved around, got a drink of water, and ate a snack, they stayed on the tree, talking to me. This was amazing, as they were only a few feet from my face.

A few nights after this encounter with the tanagers, I was visited by a spiritual guide at around one o'clock in the morning. I was sleeping and was awakened by a white flash that filled up my bedroom with intense and blinding bright light. The light was so vivid that I could not clearly see the spiritual guide. The guide appeared to be an angel. I was not afraid and felt that an important message was going to be shared with me. The spiritual guide told me that all birds and animals, especially the tiny ones, are very important to the balance of the earth. He said that all the birds and animals are very wise and that humans can learn much wisdom from them by observing their actions in nature. He stated that each animal has special strengths, attributes, and characteristics.

The spiritual guide thanked me for listening and said that he brought me a gift. The gift he gave me was an enhanced ability to observe, listen, and communicate more clearly with all birds and animals of all sizes, especially the little ones. The spiritual guide stressed that silence while observing animals out in nature was an invaluable attribute. He said that if we are silent, messages will telepathically be given to us from the animals we are observing.

Tanagers represent the small songbirds. While these birds are small, they are mighty in that they migrate through extreme weather conditions; they build nests and raise families outdoors. In order to do this, they must be wise and tenacious. Songbirds with their beautiful songs and sounds remind us about the importance of music and being joyous in all that we do, even if it is challenging. These small birds also know when to be silent and remind us that silence is equally as important as sound. They tell us that even the small things in life are important, perhaps more important than the big things in life.

Meditation with the Tanagers

Call upon tanagers to assist you when you want to play and find joy in your life and work.

Imagine that you are sitting comfortably facing west in a beautiful mountain meadow with colorful wildflowers. Close your eyes and visualize songbirds singing and flying toward you. As they get closer, you will see that they are tanagers, beautiful yellow and red songbirds. See or feel a tanager coming toward you and merging with you at your heart chakra center. Feel the warmth of the meadow and listen to the songbird. State your prayers and intentions. Ask for a message of joy from the tanager. Sit this way as long as you wish and communicate with the tanager. Be ready to feel joy and be lifted to new heights. Always thank the tanager when you are finished.

Chapter 5:
Crow Medicine

The crow family was beautiful, with the mother and father crow tending to the three baby crows. The parent crows would proudly attempt to teach the baby crows to fly daily. It was quite a show to watch the baby crows teeter on the branches of the large maple tree. As each day passed, their flight attempts improved, and they were starting to fly to the ground and gather their own seeds to eat. Their nest was in a large maple tree next to the business complex where I worked. Bill, one of the staff members in the business office on the second floor, was irritated with the crows because they made a lot of noise as they taught the baby crows to fly and gather food. Bill wanted the city to either remove or poison the crow family. I panicked at the thought of this beautiful crow family being poisoned!

I suggested to Bill that perhaps the crows liked being by the building, and I shared a lot of information about crows. I told him how they teach their babies to fly. I explained how clever they are by letting the cars smash the acorns and then swooping down to gather the smashed acorns for food. I suggested to Bill that the crow might be one of his power animal guides. I went so far as to say that he might find a crow feather when he was taking his daily walk.

I thought to myself, *Now you have done it, he might not find a feather!* At this point, I prayed to the Creator to bring Bill a feather on his daily walk. My prayer was answered! I came back from my lunch one day and there was a large, gorgeous crow feather lying on my desk. I knew that Bill had left it on my desk. He stopped by later to get his feather and said he found it on the side of the trail on his daily walk. He softened and said that he canceled his request to destroy the crows.

Two years later, long after I had forgotten about the crow family, one of my medicine teachers was conducting a reading with me regarding my power animals. She shared with me that during her shamanic journey, a crow appeared to her. The crow told her to tell me that the crow, specifically a Northwestern crow, was a new power animal for me because I had saved the lives of the crow family several years ago. I was surprised and thrilled. I had forgotten about saving the crow family.

It was so amazing to have someone else go on a shamanic journey for me and tell me about an actual past event in my life! The revelation came back full circle to me, connecting a shamanic journey reading in another dimension right back to me in my current world. This was very validating about the accuracy of information obtained in readings and shamanic journeys. This demonstrated how closely connected we are to the animals and that they truly know what is going on with us humans, and that they want to assist us. Since that time, I have had many adventures and communications with my crow power animal as well as crows of all types.

Crows represent keen discernment of everything around them and always try to communicate to us to stop and look at the whole picture of what is going on in our lives. They are shape-shifters and very clever. Crows can assist you with seeing the truth and surviving during rough times in your life. Crows can give you specific messages about events that are going to happen in the future. They can connect you to spirits that wish to speak to you from the other spiritual realms. Some people have a fear that crows convey only negative messages related to death. I have not had this experience. Black is their color, and black represents Mother Earth and the void, the place of birthing and rebirthing. Crows remind us that we can be reborn continually, and on each rebirth, we can advance to a higher and closer relationship with Mother/Father Creator. Crows survive in big cities alongside millions of people and industry, showing us that we can survive as well in all conditions.

Crows often convey messages of illness or possible death of a relative or friend. For example, a crow will always visit my sister when she needs to know if someone close to her is sick. One time she was driving in her car and a crow flew alongside her car for a mile. The crow flew at the same level as her face, right outside her car window, and looked continually into her eyes until she could feel that a message would soon be communicated to her. When my sister arrived home, there was a message on her telephone that her father-in-law was very ill. This has happened several times to my sister regarding other family members.

Crows also visit my sister-in-law at her house, telepathically communicating to her to contact me regarding her health or a family matter. They tell her if she needs to have a healing from me or if she needs to discuss a certain topic with me. It is amazing how clearly the crows communicate to her.

Meditation with Crow

Call upon crow to assist you when you want to see the whole picture of what is going on in your life for a specific situation or dilemma. Ask crow for a new or clever way to look at the situation to assist you in solving it and to be able to cope with what is happening in your life.

Sit facing east, or even better yet, sit inside a medicine wheel facing east. Close your eyes and visualize a pathway in front of you facing east. Through your heart chakra, feel crow, smell crow, stroke crow's head. With a drum or rattle, or even using your hands on your knee, beat a rhythm that feels like the heartbeat of crow. See or feel crow flying toward you and merging with you at your heart chakra center. Look into crow's eyes. State your prayers and intentions. Sit this way as long as you wish and communicate with crow. Be ready to see the whole picture and a new pathway. Always thank crow when you are finished.

CHAPTER 6:
Rattlesnake Energy

My sister Mary was frozen with fear! She was nailing up a sign on a fence when a rattlesnake slithered across her boot.

She tried to stay motionless, but in that effort she lost her balance and fell toward the large black boulders that she had been walking on by the fence line. As she fell, she could see that she was going to land right on top of the snake.

After falling, Mary tried to catch her breath, as she had the wind knocked out of her. She could feel something on her left arm. She looked down and saw that the rattlesnake's head was resting on her forearm. The hammer she had used earlier was still in her right hand, and she instinctively struck at the rattlesnake's head. She missed the snake and hit her arm instead. Writhing with great pain from the hammer's blow, she sat up, grabbing her arm.

Then suddenly Mary heard the rattling of the snake close by and simultaneously saw the snake coiling up right in front of her face.

Because she was sitting on the ground holding her arm, the snake was at the same level as her face. She was quite certain that she was going to be bitten by the snake in the face. She caught her breath and stared into the snake's eyes. She could feel that the snake was as scared as she was. She just relaxed and continued to look into the snake's eyes. The snake softened its coil and then miraculously uncoiled and retreated.

Mary was very grateful at this change of events. The few seconds staring into the snake's eyes and feeling the snake's energy was a once-in-a-lifetime experience. My sister felt that this experience would bring some major changes into her life. She did receive a new job within the next year, moved and purchased a new house.

Characteristics/Messages

Rattlesnake energy is very powerful and quick. Rattlesnakes are connected closely to Mother Earth and the element of earth. Because rattlesnakes shed their skin on a regular basis, they represent rebirthing or making changes in your lifestyle and ways of thinking. Rattlesnake energy can spiral through your body very quickly; it is a great healing energy. This energy can raise your intuitive vibratory level to new heights of clear vision and enlightenment.

Meditation with Rattlesnake

Call upon rattlesnake to assist you when you want to change your pathway and be reborn into a new way of looking at life. Rattlesnake will help you make significant changes to your lifestyle, especially your spiritual pathway. You can also call upon rattlesnake energy to purge and then heal your body.

Sit facing south. Close your eyes and visualize a pathway in front of you facing south. Through your heart chakra, feel rattlesnake energy spiraling from the earth through your feet and through the base of your spine to the top of your head. Focus on rattlesnake energy and feel the energy at your heart chakra center. State your prayers and intentions for a physical and spiritual healing. Feel new energy again spiraling through your body as you start to be reborn and heal your body. Be ready to find your true spiritual pathway. Sit this way as long as you wish and communicate with rattlesnake. Always thank rattlesnake when you are finished.

Chapter 7:
Great Horned Owl Protection

My friend Jack was terrified and did not know what he was going to do to solve his problem. Jack had accidentally witnessed a murder and was beside himself about what to do. He decided to take a walk to think about the situation. He walked through a beautiful mountain meadow and traversed his way to the edge of the great ponderosa pine trees at an elevation of over 3,000 feet; he was shaking with fear. He sat down on the ground and started praying to the Creator, asking for a solution to his dilemma and a safe pathway. For you see, Jack felt that he would be pursued by the people he had seen committing the crime. He knew he must report the murder to the police, but at this point, he was too afraid to contact the police.

When he first sat down on the ground, he noticed a huge bird flying toward him from about a mile away. The bird looked like a dot in the sky because of the far distance, but he could tell it was large. Next he saw the bird land on the top of one of the ponderosa pine trees, but it was still about four hundred feet away.

Jack bent his head down and started into deep prayer, asking for protection and for an answer to his problem. After a few minutes, he put his head up to look around and was startled to see the large bird, now only twenty feet away. It was a beautiful, huge great horned owl. Jack looked into the eyes of the owl and made spiritual and communicative contact with it. Next the owl quickly snatched a mouse from the ground and held it in its mouth. Then in two quick abrupt bites, the owl devoured the mouse.

Chills ran up and down Jack's spine, but the owl had clearly answered his inquiry and prayer. The message my friend received telepathically from the owl was that the problem could be resolved; watching the great horned owl swallow the mouse in two swift bites, Jack realized that his problem would go away quickly. My friend bowed his head in gratitude, for only a second, but when he raised his head, the owl had already disappeared.

When Jack returned back home, he heard that the people involved in the crime had been arrested. The protective energy from the great horned owl stayed with my friend for several days, and he realized that the owl was his power animal totem guide.

Characteristics/Messages

Owl is often called the night eagle. Owl is the bird of shadows and the nighttime. Because owls fly silently, they can swoop down unsuspectingly on prey. Owls have exceptional hearing abilities, enabling them to locate prey in absolute darkness. Owl can enable you to receive and see insights into the dark mysteries of life and to see through ignorance and chaos. Owl can help you have keen hearing so that you can hear things being said which most people would miss.

Meditation with Owl

Call upon owl to help you to see the truth by seeing through fear, darkness, chaos, and untruths. Owl can help you see the whole picture of what is going on in your life and show you how to carefully discern and keenly hear what messages you need to receive.

Sit facing north. Close your eyes and visualize a pathway in front of you. Through your heart chakra, feel owl and see owl flying toward you until you are looking into owl's eyes. You can visualize any species of owl you wish. With a drum or rattle, or even using your hands on your knee, beat a rhythm that feels like the heartbeat of your owl. See or feel owl coming toward you and merging with you at your heart chakra center. Look into owl's eyes. State your prayers and intentions. Ask for wisdom from owl for a certain situation or ask for a spiritual message for your highest divine good. Sit this way as long as you wish and communicate with owl. Be ready to see in all directions. Always thank owl when you are finished.

CHAPTER 8:
The Great Pyrenees Dog

Kingford, a Great Pyrenees, was my sister Mary's companion for several years. She raised him from a puppy, and he accompanied her everywhere, particularly to our family's beautiful mountain ranch. One Fourth of July, Mary and Kingford traveled to the ranch and stayed overnight in the cabin.

Very early the next morning, my sister woke to hear Kingford frantically barking outside the cabin. Mary was quite slow to get out of bed. She called to Kingford and said that she was coming, but the dog would not stop barking. She heard him run away from the cabin, still barking intensely.

Mary finally opened the door and looked out toward the pasture. To her amazement, she saw the huge white dog climbing up the corral fences. For you see, Kingford was penned into the cabin area and normally could not go through the tightly constructed corral fencing. Kingford climbed the corral fencing like it was a ladder in his desperate attempt to get out to the pasture. Why was he trying so hard to get out to the pasture?

Mary looked into the pasture and saw three cougars that had surrounded one of the horses. The horse, a wild mustang called Little Horse, was around thirty years old. He was the last horse that our father had caught and trained. Because the horse was elderly, he seemed to be an easy prey for the cougars. But Kingford loved Little Horse and was going to defend him, no matter what!

Before Mary could get out to the pasture, Kingford had climbed over two sets of corral fencing, and this was quite a feat for a dog this large. He ran out toward the cougars on a dead run to save Little Horse. The cougars turned and saw Kingford. They were trying to decide if they should take on this huge dog or flee.

By this time, Mary had also appeared in the pasture area. Her appearance, along with Kingford's aggression, convinced the cougars to flee for the forest. Mary went out to Little Horse and checked the damage. Yes, the cougars had knocked the horse down on the ground and had taken several large bites of flesh from his neck and back area. Mary was able to get Little Horse up and led him back to the barnyard area. She called me up, and I brought some antibiotics to give the horse for infection and for the bites.

For the next two weeks, Kingford would not leave Little Horse's side. He slept and ate with him until the horse recovered. Mary sent this story into the National Pyrenees Foundation, and Kingford was awarded a certificate of honor for his bravery and protection of Little Horse.

Characteristics/Messages

Dogs represent unconditional loyalty and protection for humans, other animals, and the earth. They guard us and the earth from predators, fear, and mistrust. They are fearless and will literally die for us in order to protect us. They are our best friends and companions, and do not ask anything in return from us for their loyalty. Dogs display major self-confidence in a trauma or emergency situation.

Meditation with Dog

Call upon your wonderful friend, dog, to assist you when you want your pathway protected and when you desire the attributes of self-confidence and fearlessness.

Sit facing south. Close your eyes and visualize a pathway in front of you facing south. Through your heart chakra, feel dog, smell dog, stroke dog's head. With a drum or rattle, or even using your hands on your knee, beat a rhythm that feels like the heartbeat of dog. See or feel dog coming toward you and merging with you at your heart chakra center. Look into dog's eyes. State your prayers and intentions. Sit this way as long as you wish and communicate with your special friend. Be prepared to feel safe and know that your pathway is being guarded. Always thank dog when you are finished.

Chapter 9:
The Dragonfly: Is It an Illusion?

A very special friend was distraught and had given up on her life. Alice had just received a very disappointing letter that affected how she was going to live her life. She needed to get away to think about it all. She had driven to a small lake to try to recover and was resting on the green meadow bank that surrounded the lake. Beautiful cobalt blue dragonflies were flying closely around her as she reflected on what had just happened to her. It was a glorious day, and she just wanted to be happy and content with life.

The letter stated that she had not been selected for a very important position at a local university. This was the fourth time Alice had applied at the university and was not selected. She was very well qualified and had successfully served the university in the past in a similar position for over twenty years. She had left this position to serve as a leader in the state government. She worked for four years and completed this job successfully as well. She had assisted with the passage of important legislation that improved the pay scales for women and blue collar workers. This legislation was hailed by state workers as a victory.

It was now time for Alice to return home and resume working at the university. She realized that some of the people at the university, people who could influence her selection for a job, were envious of her past accomplishments. Some of them were afraid that she would make changes at the university that would not be in their best interest. This all seemed unfair to her, as her intentions were always good and she had served the university well in the past. How could this be happening to her? She desperately needed a job at this time in her life.

Alice became very drowsy at this point and was so stressed that she dozed off into a dream. When she woke up several hours later, she felt as if she were covered with a thin and elegant blanket of some sort. When she looked down at her body, she was covered with hundreds and hundreds of the cobalt blue dragonflies. She didn't jump up or move because they were so beautiful, and there was a special essence about the dragonflies that made her feel safe and enfolded in love and kindness. She was absolutely amazed that the dragonflies were just peacefully adorning her entire body.

Alice knew there was a special and deep message for her from the dragonflies. She could feel it. She quietly searched her heart and soul for such a message. She closed her eyes again and sank into a deep meditation. The message from the dragonflies was crystal clear. They said to her, "It is all an illusion! You think the only place you should be working is at the university. This thinking is an illusion! If you will just take a few steps back, relax, and look at the whole picture of your life and its possibilities, new doors of opportunity will open. A new reality will reveal itself to you. You are trying to control the reality in your life by thinking you can only work at the university. You, in your human form, create illusions in your life by having tunnel vision and trying to control the outcome of everything in your life."

My dear friend followed the advice of the dragonflies. She relaxed and started pursuing other possibilities. She continued to apply for employment, but she sent her resume to new companies and organizations. The results were amazing. New doors of opportunity were opened to her. Within a few weeks, Alice had a new job, and within a few years, she was once again very successful.

Characteristics/Messages

Dragonflies help us to see through illusions, and yet at the same time, they remind us of balance. The shape of a dragonfly is somewhat similar to the shape of a cross. A cross can have many meanings, and one meaning is balance. The wings of the dragonfly represent balance in flight. When a person is balanced in all areas of his or her life, he or she is not easily tricked into seeing illusions and can usually find the truth in most situations. If dragonfly comes into your life, it will assist you in finding the truth and seeing beyond illusions and deceptions.

Meditation with Dragonfly

Call upon dragonfly to assist you when you want to see the truth and receive clarity about a certain situation. Ask dragonfly to remove any tricks or illusions that prevent you from seeing clearly.

Sit facing east. Close your eyes and visualize a pathway in front of you facing east. Through your heart chakra, feel dragonfly's energy. See or feel a beautifully colored dragonfly flying toward you and merging with you at your heart chakra center. State your prayers and intentions. Sit this way as long as you wish and communicate with dragonfly. Be prepared to see past any illusions. Always thank dragonfly when you are finished.

CHAPTER 10:
Eagle Medicine: Perfect Balance

Early one spring, I was meditating on the top of a beautiful mountain ridge at about 3,000 feet elevation. The wildflowers were all abloom with vibrant colors—yellow buttercups, pink bitterroot, purple wild iris, indigo blue lupines, white yarrow, white sweet potato, and camas. I loved this high spot because I could see in all four directions, and I could observe all of nature around me and below me in the meadow areas. A wide array of songbirds were flying about and singing their songs. The sun was shining, and there was a slight breeze. I could hear the water bubbling in the creek below me as I sat and merged with Mother Earth. I realized that the four elements—earth, air, water, and fire (the sun)—were with me.

I started my meditation by asking for a message to be shown to me regarding the difference between the feeling of female and male energy within my body and energy field. I wanted to discern how each energy felt, and I wanted assistance with merging them together physically and spiritually to attain an equal balance of the female and male energy.

I closed my eyes but then had an instinct to open them again, and I looked upward. Above me appeared two large bald eagles. They were soaring gracefully above me in a playful manner. They seemed to be dancing with each other in the sky. As I observed them for several minutes, I realized that they were a pair, male and female eagles. The female eagle moved in a lighter, more graceful manner, swooping downward toward me. I received a message from her telepathically to merge with her and feel the style and rhythm of her movements. Her movements were light and airy, yet strong. The essence of the female eagle was nurturing and filled with love.

Next, the male eagle swooped downward toward me, and I was guided to merge with him. His movements were of a more deliberate and stronger nature. I could feel support and stability from him.

Next, the two eagles flew side by side, and their movements became as one. They demonstrated a perfect synchronization of movement. The essence coming from both of them at this point was oneness, love, balance, and strength.

I realized that I could now discern between male and female energy using the eagle movements as my baseline. I next closed my eyes and felt into my own female and male energies. I merged them together at my heart center and honored both energies.

When I opened my eyes, the eagles were now perched about two hundred feet from me, on a high rock cropping on a nearby ridge. They were observing everything in all directions around them. It was magnificent to be so close to these awesome birds, and I could feel a calmness coming from them. They continued to look in all directions, above and below, and in the four directions of east, south, west, and north. Telepathically, I was getting energy and information from them. I sat and merged with them and their energy. What came next was a wonderful message regarding illumination. The eagles demonstrated how they fly to a high point, like the top of a tree or rock cropping, to see the whole picture of what is happening. If the eagles are distressed in any way, they fly to the highest point to regain their stability and see the whole picture. This is the essence of illumination. What a wonderful message, and one that I have used over and over in my lifetime to recover from distress. Instead of reacting to a distressing situation, I pause, look at the whole picture, and then I can become proactive, instead of reactive, in solving and responding to the situation.

Next, I received a message from the eagles to share this teaching with others. I was asked to guide others to fly with the eagles, first with the female eagle, feeling into her energy and movements, and then with the male eagle, feeling into his energy and movements. The next step is to merge the female and male eagles and then soar as one eagle in perfect balance and harmony.

Characteristics/Messages

Eagles represent balance, strength, illumination, discernment, peace, and joy. They are divine messengers to the Creator. They deliver our prayers and affirmation to the heavens and the Creator. They can assist you in soaring to new heights in all areas of your life. They give us the gift of illumination or being able to see the whole picture of what is going on in our life for a given situation or dilemma.

Call upon eagle to assist you when you want to see the whole picture of what is going on in your life regarding a certain situation. Ask eagle to help you to make a wise decision. Ask eagle to carry your affirmations and prayers to the Creator.

Sit facing east. Close your eyes and visualize a pathway in front of you facing east. With a drum or rattle, or even using your hands on your knee, beat a rhythm that feels like the heartbeat of eagle. See or feel eagle flying toward you and merging with you at your heart chakra center. Look into eagle's eyes. Ask eagle to take you to the top of a large tree, where you can reflect and look out over a beautiful landscape. State your prayers and intentions. Sit this way as long as you wish and communicate with eagle. Be prepared to receive the gift of illumination. Always thank eagle when you are finished.

CHAPTER 11:
Red-Tailed Hawk Energy

The red-tailed hawk was very large, fully mature, and gorgeous in color; it soared above my car as I drove on the country road on my way home from work on a beautiful summer evening. There were two baby red-tailed hawks soaring by the larger hawk. The larger red-tailed hawk was then joined by another mature red-tailed hawk. It became clear that this was a red-tailed hawk family.

Suddenly, one of the mature hawks soared too close to a power line and hit the wire. The hawk fell abruptly onto the roadside. I waited to see if the hawk would recover and fly away. It did not move. A man driving toward me saw the injured hawk on the roadside. To my dismay, he got out of his car and started kicking at the hawk to move it from the roadway. I told the man that I was experienced with wildlife and that I would move the hawk (sigh, I was not experienced at all, but I could not tolerate his treatment of the beautiful red-tailed hawk). Fortunately, the man got back in his car and drove off.

By this time, the other parent hawk and two baby hawks were screeching overhead, obviously distressed. I walked up to the wounded hawk and could see that it was alive and trying to fly. The hawk could walk, but its left wing was injured. I called a local veterinarian, who is very experienced with birds, and asked for someone to come from his office.

While I waited for help, I began talking to the red-tailed hawk. I was amazed when the hawk looked straight into my eyes with a kind look of appreciation. At this instant, I knew the hawk was the mother hawk of the family. Her eyes were a deep golden brown color, and her energy essence was very loving, kind, and powerful. We merged energetically and telepathically. Her message was that while she was grateful for my help, she was hurt badly and would not return to her family. She asked me to explain this to the father red-tailed hawk and their babies.

I began to communicate to the baby hawks and father hawk that they would have to continue without the mother hawk. I told them that she would be taken care of but would not be able to fly and return to them. I asked the father hawk to continue raising the baby hawks and told him he would be successful. The father and baby hawks seemed to listen as they perched on an elm tree above me.

The veterinarian assistant arrived at the scene and was very helpful. She could see that the mother red-tailed hawk was severely injured. She carefully picked up the hawk and put it in a carrier in the back of her vehicle. She said she would call me with the status of the mother hawk's condition.

I lovingly said good-bye to the mother red-tailed hawk. The hawk looked deeply into my eyes, and our hearts merged with loving energy.

She telepathically told me that her loving energy would always be with me and that I could communicate with her in the future in the spiritual realms.

It has been over four years since the mother red-tailed hawk passed on to the heavens, and I still communicate with this amazing bird whenever she appears in my mediations and journeys. She has given me advice and strength over the years on many topics. I soar with her in the sky whenever I need to do so in order to gain strength and see the whole picture of what is happening with a particular situation in my life. For you see, she has given me the gifts of illumination, love, strength, and faith. I can call on her anytime, feel her energy, and telepathically communicate with her.

And by the way, the father red-tailed hawk successfully raised the baby hawks. He made the most of his life by demonstrating strength and love for his family. He recently found a new female red-tailed hawk mate and has raised several other families. What an example for humanity!

Characteristics/Messages

Red-tailed hawks are leaders and pioneers; they show the way of spiritual pathways! They have high energy and will not stop until they have reached their goal. They are also acrobats and love attention. If you talk to them, they often will fly lower and closer to you, and they will communicate both verbally and telepathically with you. They will give you the gifts of strength, endurance, fearlessness, and illumination.

Call upon red-tailed hawk to assist you when you want to see the whole picture of what is going on for a specific situation or dilemma. Ask red-tailed hawk for the qualities of fearlessness and strength.

Sit facing the direction of east. Close your eyes and visualize a pathway in front of you facing east. Through your heart chakra, feel red-tailed hawk's energy. With a drum or rattle, or even using your hands on your knee, beat a rhythm that feels like the heartbeat of red-tailed hawk. See or feel a red-tailed hawk flying toward you and merging with you at your heart chakra center. Look into the red-tailed hawk's eyes. Send her love and appreciation. State your prayers and intentions. Sit this way as long as you wish and communicate with the red-tailed hawk. Be prepared to feel energized and to receive the gift of strength and illumination. Always thank red-tailed hawk when you are finished.

CHAPTER 12:
Bear:
Spiritual Pathway Connector

My wonderful spirit sister and friend, Kathleen, shared with me several years ago a message she received while she was deep in meditation in a shamanic journey. In her journey, a black bear appeared to her and left a message with her to share with me later when she finished her journey. Kathleen called me on the telephone and shared with me the following message from black bear.

Black bear appeared to Kathleen and told her that he was one of my power animal guides. He said that he would show me my spiritual pathway and assist me with my spiritual classes and healing sessions. He said that he would give me the good medicine of physical endurance so that my body could stay in a meditative state for long periods of time. Bear said that he would guide many people to my spiritual classes to connect with my spiritual teachings.

Since Kathleen shared this message with me, bear has been my constant companion whenever I drum shamanic journeys for myself and others. Bear is a guide of spiritual and service pathways—pathways that give us joy. Bear assists me with interpreting messages from my meditations and shamanic journeys for myself and others. Bear believes that each person has a special spiritual pathway that will bring them joy, peace, truth, wisdom, and love. Bear asks us to find joy in our careers and in our service to others on earth. Bear says that if we are not happy with our career choice, we should find a new career that is rewarding.

Characteristics/Messages

Bear medicine is the ability to find your service pathway, the pathway that truly gives you joy. Your service pathway includes both your spiritual and career pathways. Bears are always very clear about their pathway and intentions. They will not let anyone or anything stop or divert them when they are following their true pathway. Bears represent strength and endurance, and they never give up on life, no matter what happens to them. They are great parents and communicators.

Bear medicine also gives us the powerful gift of introspection and discernment while dreaming, meditating, or shamanically journeying. Bear can awaken our unconscious and connect us to the messages meant for us through our soul.

Meditation with Bear

Call upon bear to assist you with finding your spiritual and career pathway so you can find joy in your life. Or you may call upon bear to assist you with connecting to your inner self and spiritual guides while meditating, dreaming, or journeying.

Sit facing west. Close your eyes and visualize a pathway in front of you facing west. Through your heart chakra, feel bear's energy. With a drum or rattle, or even using your hands on your knee, beat a rhythm that feels like the heartbeat of bear. See or feel bear walking toward you and merging with you at your heart chakra center. Look into bear's eyes. State your prayers and intentions. Be prepared to receive the gifts of strength, joy, and introspection from deep within yourself. Sit this way as long as you wish and communicate with bear. Always thank bear when you are finished.

Chapter 13:
Frog Medicine: The Element of Water

On May 18, 1980, Mary and Jim, my brother-in-law, were caught in a thick fog of ash from Mount St. Helens, which had just erupted earlier that day. When the volcano erupted, they were on horseback checking range fences on the ranch, at an elevation of about 3,500 feet. They were miles away from the ranch's cabin. They could not even see each other due to the thick volcanic ash. The horses were so scared they started to jump and buck. Mary and Jim had to dismount, unsaddle the horses, and let them go free. They tried to walk back to the cabin, but it was almost impossible, as they could not even see the ground below them. They tied their two jackets together and held onto them so that they would not become separated.

They knew to walk downhill, as the cabin was located at the south end of the ranch. They eventually found one of the range fences and followed it for several miles. They fell down continually. Mary ran into a tree limb, and it impaled her shoulder. Jim had to help pull it out.

They eventually lit all the matches they had to help them see their path. They burnt up all the paper articles they had in their wallets, even their money, in order to assist them with walking toward the cabin.

They were getting desperate, as their drinking water was gone. They were getting exhausted, and the volcanic ash was caking their mouth, teeth, and throats. All of a sudden, they heard galloping and realized that a herd of horses from the ranch were running toward them with fear. The horses ran over the top of them, leaving them grappling on the ground. Luckily, no bones were broken from the horses trampling them.

They were exhausted and could hardly breathe due to the thick ash. They were incredibly thirsty. Mary was not sure if she was going to survive this situation.

They continued their journey, hoping to find the cabin and water. Mary started hearing a faint sound. She listened carefully and realized that the sound was frogs croaking. She became excited because she knew the frogs must be in the pond by the cabin. She had never heard them croak so loudly before, but she was so thankful that her prayers were being answered for assistance to find water and the cabin. She and Jim walked toward the sounds coming from the frogs. They could tell they were getting closer; the croaking sounds became louder with each step. It took them about two hours of walking, falling down, getting up, and then pushing themselves forward until finally, they walked into the yard area of the cabin and could feel one of the walls of the cabin. They found the door, went inside, and thankfully drank glass after glass of water.

After a while, Mary went out to the pond and sat down and listened to the frogs. Their croaking was like music, and she thanked them over and over again for guiding her to the cabin and safety.

Characteristics/Messages

Frogs are the great communicators. They bless and bring forth the element of water and can control the weather. Frogs are transformers and can give us the gift of metamorphosis—the ability to change to suit any given situation. The frogs certainly communicated and guided Mary and Jim back home and gave them the ability to change to survive the volcanic eruption.

Meditation with Frog

Call upon frog to assist you in finding your pathway, even when there are extreme obstacles in your way. Frog will lead you to the truth and right answers to your questions and dilemmas. Frog will show what changes, or metamorphosis, is necessary to be successful.

Sit facing west, the direction of the element water. Close your eyes and visualize a pathway in front of you. Through your heart chakra, feel frog and see frog guiding you down the pathway. As you follow frog, merge with the energy of frog at your heart chakra center. With a drum or rattle, or even using your hands on your knee, beat a rhythm that feels like the heartbeat of frog. Frog may even lead you to a stream or pond where you and frog will enter and float in the water. Relax and go with the flow. State your prayers and intentions. Ask for wisdom from frog for a certain situation or ask for a spiritual message for your highest divine good. Ask for your pathway to be cleared so that you can see clarity and truth. Sit this way as long as you wish and communicate with frog. Be prepared for a change to take place in your life. Always thank frog when you are finished.

PART TWO:

Personal Growth

CHAPTER 14:
Preparing for Your Journey

Who are you? How do you start on your spiritual pathway? You are a beautiful spiritual being. There are four parts to your being: physical, mental, emotional, and spiritual. Your spiritual being is your soul. It is desirable to have these four parts of your being all in alignment, or in oneness with your spiritual pathway. In other words, your physical, mental, and emotional parts should be in oneness with your spiritual soul. Your soul is who you really are and can guide you to make decisions that are in your highest interest. Your soul has experienced other lifetimes and stores divine wisdom to share with you.

Awakening to Your Inner Wisdom and Spiritual Pathway

Wisdom begins from within: learning, listening, knowing, and respecting oneself. Many of us have forgotten how to learn from within and how to communicate with our soul. With a little practice, we can quickly reawaken ourselves and start communicating with our soul and our spirit guides. It is through your soul that you communicate with your spirit guides, and it is through your soul that you channel energy to heal others and yourself.

At first, you may not believe that you have spirit guides, angels, or power animals; you may not even believe you have a soul to communicate with, but you can communicate with it inwardly, through meditation and shamanic journeys. If you search deep within your heart, and when you see miracles happen every day, like the birth of a new baby, a beautiful sunset, and prayers answered, then you know that there is much, much more than just your everyday life and routines. I challenge you to believe and keep an open mind as you reconnect to your soul, your spirit guides, and God (Mother/Father Creator).

Mother/Father Creator is our main spiritual guide and created the humans, the animals, the earth, the trees, the rocks, the elements, and so forth.

Communicating and Connecting with Your Soul

Close your eyes and open your heart chakra and fill your heart area with love and appreciation. Open your heart area up like a beautiful large rose or lotus flower and see yourself seated in the middle of the flower. Pick a favorite color for your flower. Now move this energy of love down to your solar plexus chakra and open that chakra with love and appreciation. Merge the solar plexus chakra with the heart chakra. Feel your entire body filling up with love and healing energy, upward and downward from these two chakra points. Feel your entire physical body merging with your soul. See your soul as a beautiful spiritual being and see that beautiful spiritual being as yourself. Sit in silence for a few minutes, or as long as you wish, merged with your soul. Feel into any messages you are receiving from your soul. Notice how peaceful you feel throughout your body.

This is an exercise that could be done every morning, or as often as needed throughout the day, so that you are merged and communicating with your soul every second of every day. After a while, you will always be merged and in communication with your soul. You will start to notice when you are not in sync with your soul.

To assist you with meditating and focusing on your chakras, I have listed below the seven main chakras in your body. A chakra is a crystalline power center in your body that you can tap into energetically for meditating, healing, and enlightenment.

- The root or base chakra is located at the base of your spine or perineum and assists you with survival and healing of your physical body. Main color to focus on is red.
- The sacral or naval chakra is located at your naval and assists you with healing relationships (including sexual) with others. Main color to focus on is orange.
- The solar plexus chakra is located in the center of your solar plexus and assists you with healing and advancing your spirituality or spiritual pathway. Main color to focus on is yellow.
- The heart chakra is located at your heart center and assists you with finding and expressing divine love, joy, and gratitude. Main color to focus on is green.
- The throat chakra is located at the center of your throat and

assists you with clear communication of all types. Main color to focus on is blue/turquoise.

- The third eye chakra is located at the center of your forehead and assists you with clear vision and interpretation of your dreams and images while meditating. Main color to focus on is indigo blue/purple.

- The crown chakra is located at the top of your head in the center crown area. This chakra connects you to God and the celestial/angelic realms. It assists you with interpreting the outcome of messages received during dreams and meditations. Main color to focus on is amethyst.

CHAPTER 15:
Finding Your Power Animal

As I stated previously in this book, each person has at least nine power animal guides. You have a guardian power animal that has been with you since your birth. You also can have a number of power animals in addition to your guardian power animal, and they can change somewhat throughout your life. A good starting point is to think about what animal or animals you like or think about often. Power animals include insects, birds, and fish. A very small insect can be as powerful as a large animal such as the cougar or wolf. Power animals are sent to us by Mother/Father Creator to provide spiritual medicine to us. They teach us through their actions, strengths, and weaknesses when we observe them out in nature. We can receive messages from them while we are observing and communicating with them out in nature or while in meditation or on a shamanic journey. They are another form of a guardian angel for each of us.

Let's go on a meditation journey and find one of your power

animals. You can do this meditation either sitting outside in nature or inside. You may play soft music or shamanic drumming music to assist you with your journey. You may ask someone to drum for your journey, or you may drum yourself while journeying. Rattles and other instruments can be used as well.

1. Imagine that a medicine wheel (a circle of rocks) is surrounding you, or you may make one by making a circle around yourself with tobacco or cornmeal. You may use crystals and place each crystal in the four directions around yourself. The following crystals are very effective to use for the four directions:

- East: yellow or gold colored crystal or rock (amber or yellow citrine)
- South: red colored crystal or rock (red jasper, ruby)
- West: black colored crystal or rock (obsidian, onyx)
- North: white colored crystal or rock (clear quartz)

Some of you may already have created a medicine wheel on your property or in a sacred area outdoors (see the next chapter). Being inside the medicine wheel places you in sacred space and empowers your journey.

2. Open your heart and fill it with love and appreciation for all that you have and for the information you are about to receive in your journey. Close your eyes, open your third eye chakra (in the center of your forehead), and connect it to your heart chakra. Picture yourself in the center of your heart, sitting beside a big tree (pick one of your favorite trees). Slowly float down the root of the tree, deep into the center of the earth (Mother Earth). See yourself sitting in Mother Earth

by a pathway, but still connected to the root of the tree. Ask for your power animal to come down the pathway and meet you. Stay in your journey as long as you feel comfortable. When you are ready to return, float back up the root of the tree to your heart chakra center and open your eyes. Write down, in a journal, what happened in your journey and subsequent journeys.

If you are unable to discern your power animal on this first journey, don't give up. Continue to journey again and ask for your power animal. More than one power animal may appear. You may not actually see your power animal, but feel its presence and know which power animal it is. Often, a few days after your journey, you may also receive information, or a knowingness, about who your power animal is, and you may get a message as well. Keep an open mind, be flexible, and believe!

Chapter 16:
Sacred Space

Creating Your Sacred Space

Creating sacred space empowers your prayers, meditations, and journeys. Sacred space raises your vibratory level and enhances your communications with your soul and your spirit guides. It brings you closer to God (Mother/Father Creator).

You can create sacred space in any location in your home, in your yard or garden, or out in nature. Your sacred space can be secretive, or it can be a space you create to share with your family and others.

There are a number of ways to create sacred space around you. I will share some of the main ways, but feel free to enhance these and create whatever type of sacred space you wish.

One way is to place a medicine wheel around you prior to starting your prayers, meditations, and journeys. You can do this by simply asking one to be around you, or you can make a medicine wheel with tobacco, cornmeal, crystals, rocks, or whatever sacred objects you wish. It is very desirable to build a permanent medicine wheel outside that you can regularly sit inside of to meditate and journey. When you are in this powerful circle, your prayers are amplified and your journeys are empowered.

Another way to create sacred space is to place yourself in sacred pyramid space. Imagine a square-based (four corners) golden pyramid and see yourself seated elegantly in the center of the pyramid. The top of the pyramid has an indigo blue opening that reaches high up into the upper world (the heavens). At your feet is another square-based pyramid that is inverted; the top of the pyramid has an indigo blue opening that reaches downward into the lower world (the inner earth). See yourself floating slightly downward so that your waist is at the exact location where the pyramid floors touch each other. From your waist up, you are sitting in the upper pyramid, and from your waist down, you are sitting in the lower pyramid. The four points of the bases of the pyramids represent the four directions and elements. Again, when you are in this powerful space, your prayers are amplified and your journeys are empowered.

Remember that you can include music, as it is a major way to create sacred space and raise your vibration level. Or you may drum, rattle, dance, or sing to enhance and create sacred space.

A Sacred Space Meditation

I was in deep meditation traveling upward to the heavens, the upper sacred world, to visit with the divine Mother/Father Creator. I traveled upward, upward, going as high as I could, until I felt a connection to

Mother/Father Creator, like attaching to a star in the heavens. My body felt light and feathery, and a feeling of love and appreciation filled my heart and entire body. I could see sparkling stars all around me.

A white stairway appeared, and I climbed up the stairway and opened a white door that led me into a bright white chamber; I felt the presence of Mother/Father Creator. I bowed and knelt before them, asking for a message to assist me on my spiritual path. I was handed a brilliant golden medallion. The medallion was circular and very ornate, with rose-like flowers etched on the front side of the medallion. In the center of the medallion was a circle with twelve paths leading to the center circle. Mother/Father Creator told me that this was the sacred circle of life and represented medicine wheels of all beliefs. I was told that the paths leading to the center represented the paths of all of creation, which included all the tribes and races of people on Mother Earth. The four directions—east, south, west, and north—were represented on the medallion. The four directions included all of nature, the rocks, animals, trees and plants, the four elements, and all that there is above and below Mother Earth. The center of the medallion represented Mother/Father Creator; it is the spot of oneness with all of creation. I was told to place the medallion at my heart chakra, and the essence of it would always be there as a part of my being and assist me on my spiritual path and desire to be in oneness with Mother Earth and all of creation.

I was told to share the following message: Everyone may travel upward as I have described and climb the sacred stairway to Mother/Father Creator. You will be given a gift to assist you with your spiritual pathway and a spiritual message. I encourage you to visit with Mother/Father Creator on a regular basis in this manner to receive many gifts and messages.

CHAPTER 17:
All of Creation:
Mother Earth and the Four Elements; The Trees ("The
Standing People"); The Rock People; The Two-Leggeds
(The Humans); The Sky Nation; The Thunder Beings

According to many indigenous cultures, all of creation is comprised
of seven main creations: the earth (the four elements), the standing
people (the trees), the rock people (the rocks and mountains), the
animal kingdom, the two-leggeds (the humans), the sky nation (the
stars and planets), and the thunder beings (the four elements). All of
the creations are related, and as I have stated previously, everyone and
everything is related. What happens to one creation will affect all of
the other creations. Thus, I believe it is very important to honor all of
the creations and be a good steward of the earth.

The first part of this book has already shared stories and meditations
from one of the creations, the animals. In part two, I will describe and
share information about the remaining creations.

Mother Earth and the Four Elements

Mother Earth is composed of the four elements of earth, water, fire, and air. It is very desirable for us to recognize that we, too, are part of the elements. Mother Earth is within us, and we are within her. All of creation lives on Mother Earth and is part of the earth. All of creation is equal and related. When we, the humans, abuse the earth and are not respectful of Mother Earth and her resources, we are endangering all of the other members of creation on Mother Earth. We are endangering our children's and grandchildren's ability to survive in the future.

Connecting to Mother Earth for Healing and Wisdom

Mother Earth is a divine and sacred planet, and each of us is divine and sacred. She is calling to us to respect her, the elements, nature, and all of creation on Mother Earth.

The element of earth represents wisdom, patience, and prosperity. Everything we need to survive is already on the earth. The message from Mother Earth is to start really knowing ourselves and what we need and desire to find joy and peace in our lives. Once we no longer limit ourselves by trying to mold ourselves into what we believe others think we should be, we are truly free to connect to and communicate with our own soul essence. We can then find inner wisdom and joy by following our desired pathway, not a pathway designed to please others.

The following meditation is a very powerful and wonderful way for you to connect to Mother Earth and communicate with her at a deep level. Remember that Mother Earth has a conscious spiritual essence and can communicate with you through your soul during meditation and journeys with and into Mother Earth.

Go to your heart chakra and open it wide like a beautiful rose or lotus flower. Fill your heart and your entire body with divine love energy for Mother Earth. Breathe in this divine love from your entire body/being, and then on the exhale, send the divine love energy down your spine and out your perineum and down your legs and out through the chakras in the balls of your feet into Mother Earth. Visualize Mother Earth filling up with divine love energy and light. Inhale again, this time from deep inside Mother Earth (the inner earth), back up through your feet, legs, and spine into your heart. Hold this energy and fill it with divine love energy and exhale this energy back down your legs, feet, and spine into Mother Earth. Rhythmically inhale and exhale from and into Mother Earth. You will start synchronizing with Mother Earth's breath, and you will merge and become one with Mother Earth. Both you and Mother Earth will receive healing and blessings. You may then journey down into Mother Earth and communicate with her and seek wisdom and insight. When you are done, return to your heart chakra center.

This exercise and merging with Mother Earth will stabilize both the earth and you. It will provide you with healing and blessings and will bring you into oneness with Mother Earth and all of creation on Mother Earth.

Connecting to Water for Healing and Wisdom

The element of water teaches us adaptation and assists us with our intuition, dreams, and inner vision. Adaptation, like water, teaches us to shift to meet the challenges in our life for the better. Water as an element shape-shifts through the earth, forming large rivers and lakes. It is strong enough to reshape the earth's landscape in order to reach its destination. Likewise, the element of water can assist us with our pathway in life through our dreams, journeys, and inner vision by showing us what we need to restructure in our life in order to be successful.

The following meditation is a very powerful and wonderful way for you to connect and merge with the element of water. Remember that water has a conscious spiritual essence and can communicate with you through your soul essence during meditation and journeys.

Go to your heart chakra and open it wide like a beautiful rose or lotus flower. Fill your heart and your entire body with divine love energy for the element of water. Now see yourself sitting by a beautiful stream in the mountains. The scenery is beautiful as you are sitting on lush green grass amid beautiful wildflowers. The water is bubbling beside you, and you are soaking your feet in the stream. Gently start merging your energy with the energy from the stream, and breathe rhythmically with the bubbling sound of the stream. Ask the element of water for strength and inner vision to make necessary changes in your life for your highest good. You can ask specific questions about anything you wish. Continue to merge and meditate with the element of water. Breathe in the stream's divine love energy throughout your body, and exhale divine love energy back into the stream from your body. You will start synchronizing with the flow of the water from the stream, and you will become in oneness with the stream. Both you and the element of water will receive healing and blessings. When you are done, return to your heart chakra center and thank the element of water.

Connecting to Air for Healing and Wisdom

The element of air represents unity. It connects the heavens with earth. In fact, it connects everything through the breezes. The trees, the Standing People, assist in bringing us the element of air through their leaves and branches when the breezes and winds blow around us. The element of air is part of our weather patterns, but it is so much more. For you see, the breezes and stronger winds created by air carry a spiritual consciousness and messages if we tune into them.

The element of air is contained in our physical bodies as oxygen. So when you bless the element of air, you are also blessing the parts of your body that carry this element. We cannot live without air and oxygen.

The following meditation will show you how to connect to air and stir up the breezes around you. Remember that air has a conscious spiritual essence and can communicate with you through your soul essence during meditation and journeys.

Go to your heart chakra and open it wide like a beautiful rose or lotus flower. Fill your heart and your entire body with divine love energy for the element of air. Now see yourself sitting in the center of a beautiful forest with trees of all kinds. Imagine your favorite type of tree, and see yourself leaning against the tree. Start to feel a light breeze of air blow across your cheek. Merge into the breeze and feel its energy. Start breathing in rhythm with the breeze. Continue to merge and start meditating with the sound, feel, and energy of the breeze. Ask the element of air to connect you to the wisdom that you need for a certain situation. Ask the element of air to connect you to your higher self in order to seek spiritual wisdom. Continue to merge and meditate with the element of air. Breathe in the element of air's divine love energy throughout your body, and exhale divine love energy back into the air and breeze from your body. You will start synchronizing with the flow of the air, and you will become in oneness with the breeze. You will receive wisdom, healing, and blessings. When you are done, return to your heart chakra center and thank the element of air.

Connecting to Fire for Healing and Wisdom

The element of fire represents our heart center, the center of love and passion. The fire in our heart can help us to re-create our life and seek out what is best for our highest good. Fire can burn away what is not needed in order to be reborn; it can also purify us and create a new pathway for us to follow.

The following meditation will show you how to connect with the element of fire and create your own spiritual pathway. Remember that fire has a conscious spiritual essence and can communicate with you through your soul essence during meditation and journeys.

Go to your heart chakra and open it wide like a beautiful rose or lotus flower. Fill your heart and your entire body with divine love energy for the element of fire. Now see yourself sitting by a wonderful campfire in the woods. The scenery is beautiful as you are sitting at the edge of a forest with a grand view of a mountain range in the distance. The fire is crackling beside you and inspiring your thoughts. Gently start merging your energy with the energy from the fire, and breathe rhythmically with the sound and energy coming from the fire. Ask the element of fire to purify you and create a clear spiritual pathway for you to follow. You can ask specific questions in order to seek wisdom for your highest good or to find what is your true passion in life. Continue to merge and meditate with the element of fire. Breathe in the fire's divine love energy throughout your body, and exhale divine love energy back into the fire from your body. You will start synchronizing with the rhythm of the fire, and you will become in oneness with the fire. You will receive purification, wisdom, healing, and blessings. When you are done, return to your heart chakra center and thank the element of fire.

The Trees: "The Standing People"

The Standing People are the trees. Every tree, and for that matter every plant and bush, has a spiritual essence, and we can communicate, through our soul, with them.

The trees can assist us with connecting to both the lower and upper worlds. Their roots go deep into Mother Earth and connect us to the inner-dimensional lower world, the terrestrial world. The branches reach upward and connect us to the upper world, the celestial world.

Even though trees are harvested for many reasons, their spiritual essence still remains on earth through their roots, because every tree is spiritually and energetically connected through its root system to all the other trees that inhabit the earth. The trees that are cut down are not visible to humans on the earth, but they are still alive in inner earth through their root system. This can be very comforting to those of us who have lost our beautiful trees due to logging or fires.

The Standing People silently hold the knowledge of all the civilizations that have inhabited earth. They have many sacred gifts and knowledge to offer us. They not only provide resources to us, but they offer us strength and wisdom. The Standing People are our spiritual partners and are ready to assist us on our spiritual journeys.

If you sit against or by a tree, you may journey to the tree and have questions answered. You can feel the energy from the tree, and if you are patient, you will receive information. If you touch the tree and send loving energy back to the tree, positive and loving energy will be returned to you, and you will feel the positive energy throughout your body. This can be very healing to your physical ailments. You can travel with the tree to the lower world by opening your heart chakra, see yourself in your heart sitting by the tree, and then float down a root of the tree into Mother Earth. Float way down into the center of Mother Earth. Feel and sense inner earth. You may then ask questions or just sit there and receive healing and blessings. When you are ready, float back up until you are seated back by the tree at your heart center. Then you may journey upward by floating up a branch to the top of the tree. Next allow the tree to push you way up into the upper world until you connect to a star. You may then meditate in the upper world and connect to Mother/Father Creator. You may feel the angelic realms. You may then ask questions or just sit there and receive healing and blessings. When you are ready, float back down until you are seated again by the tree at your heart center.

The Rock People

The Rock People represent all of the rocks and crystals of the earth. Rocks help hold the earth together. The beautiful mountains of earth are made of rocks and crystals. There are crystalline caves on the earth as well as in inner earth. Inner earth is the center of the earth where the water aquifers are located and where the tree roots reside. Inner earth is considered as sacred as the surface of the earth. Inner earth houses many special crystal caves and energy vortex centers such as at Mount Shasta and Mount Rainier.

Crystals and rocks can assist us with our spiritual enlightenment by holding them to our heart chakra or third eye chakra while meditating. Because each crystal has its own energy essence, crystals helps us discern our messages received during meditations. Crystals are used to enhance healings, and their color is important in the healing and meditation process. Some major crystals and colors are listed below to assist you with your special crystal meditations and journeys.

- Clear Quartz: This crystal can be used for absolutely everything, and when placed alongside any other crystal, clear quartz amplifies the power of the other crystal. Clear quartz is great for physical healings as well as for enhancing your ability to discern spiritual messages. This crystal helps open up the crown chakra. Color is clear to smoky white.
- Amethyst: This crystal enhances your ability to discern and see spiritual messages while journeying. It helps open up the third eye chakra and crown chakra. Color is light lavender into purple.
- Malachite: This is a powerful healing rock especially for the throat area and finding clear communication. It also assists with creative endeavors and attracting success and wealth. Color is vivid green with black swirls occurring on some rocks.
- Rose Quartz: This crystal enhances your ability to feel divine love at the heart center and throughout the body. It helps heal

a broken heart and is good for overall body healing. Color is light pink into darker pinks.

- Tiger Eye: This crystal helps the solar plexus chakra to open and assists you with discerning your dreams and meditations. It connects you deeply to your soul. It can be worn as a necklace or placed in a pocket or medicine bag to attract prosperity. Color is yellow into golden browns.
- Orange Citrine: This crystal assists with opening up the sacral chakra located at the navel and removing any negative energy or negative entities from the body. It assists with enhancing your relationship with others. Color is orange.
- Red Jasper: This is a great rock to use for physical healing, especially if placed on the root chakra. It can also be carried in your pocket or worn as a necklace for protection. Color is red.
- Obsidian: This crystal absorbs negative energies and removes them from the body. Can also be used to connect one to the void of Mother Earth for rebirthing and new beginnings. Color is black.

The Two-Leggeds (The Humans)

The people of the earth, the two-leggeds or the humans, are the guardians of the earth and all of creation on the earth. Their main responsibility should be to care for the earth, animals, nature, their children, each other, and so forth.

Because the humans have constructed so many houses and continue to develop nature and green areas on the earth, I believe the future survival of earth and the humans could truly be in jeopardy.

The animals are attempting to communicate with the humans in many ways to give them the message to stop polluting and overdeveloping earth.

Animals are moving into cities to show the humans that they have taken their habitat away. Animals are coming into the meditations and dreams of the humans to spiritually connect with them and convey these messages. The animals are reminding the humans that they are spiritual beings who can communicate with the animals telepathically and through meditations. The animals are reminding the humans to partner with the animals to heal and balance all of creation on the earth.

The Sky Nation

The Sky Nation (Father Sky) represents our galaxy of planets and the stars, also often called the Star Nation by many indigenous cultures. It is believed by many cultures, such as Native Americans, that we are seeded from the stars. In other words, our origin is from the stars in such locations as the Pleiades and Orion's Belt, the star Sirius, and the North Star, to name a few. The Sky Nation provides the atmosphere around earth and the other planets. Thus, it is important to take care of the atmospheric layers around earth. Earth and the sky are related, as is everything and everyone. What happens to one will affect the other in some manner.

The Sky Nation is where the celestial energies reside, and when one meditates and connects to the stars, one can feel these high-level energies as well as have experiences with one's angel guides. Connecting through meditation and journeying to the sky and stars enhances one's ability to feel the God (Mother/Father Creator) energy and to pray and talk with God.

The Thunder Beings

The Thunder Beings represent the rain, wind, and thunder and lightning storms that cleanse the earth. The Thunder Beings contain the four elements of earth, air, water, and fire. Thunder storms bring water in the form of rain or hail to the earth, and lightning brings fire to the earth. Lightning cleanses the earth and the waters of the earth. The element of air creates the wind storms that occur with the thunder storms. While a thunder and lightning storm can be scary and worrisome, the earth is usually greener and feels refreshed after the storm.

The Thunder Beings are considered to be spiritual emissaries who can appear and bring messages of truth during one's meditation or journey. Their messages are deep and profound, like a strong wind and rain storm. The Thunder Beings represent truth and often foretell that a powerful change is coming soon.

CHAPTER 18:
The Power of Your Thoughts and Prayers

If we realized that every one of our thoughts is a form of prayer and is heard by Mother/Father Creator, we would be more conscious of our thinking patterns. Our thinking patterns create what comes into our lives and affects our lives in every way imaginable. You create that which you think. Thinking of someone or something creates a thought form that is sent out into the universe. I am sure you have had the experience of thinking about someone and then they either call you on the telephone or visit you in person. So you can see that it is important to send out positive and loving thoughts and energy, because what you send out through thoughts is what is returned back to you.

Prayers are thoughts that are put into words with intensity and feeling. When intensity and feeling are added to prayers, it raises the vibratory level of the thought patterns, and they travel faster and further. Thoughts conveyed through prayer can manifest faster in our lives. Realize that you are a co-creator with Mother/Father Creator and that you can manifest what you wish for into your life.

Do not waste one more moment of your life. Believe you are a co-creator with God. See your abundance, not your lack. Ask and pray for that which enhances your life, your family's life, and all of creation on earth.

Chapter 19:
Losing a Pet

It is really overwhelming to lose our pets and special animal friends to death. But I want to assure you that when they pass on, their soul is taken to Mother/Father Creator and their soul (spirit) continues to live. You can bring your pet back to yourself through your heart and soul by calling them to your heart and feeling their energy presence with you. If you sit quietly, close your eyes, and ask them to come, you will be able to feel their energy and presence with you, and you can even see them, with your eyes closed, through your third-eye chakra (located in the center of your forehead). In this way, they can be with you when you are hiking, meditating, or whenever you want to call them and feel them with you through your heart. If you are meditating or journeying and you call them to be with you, you will be able to communicate with them through the spiritual realms.

Conclusion

The power animals and I would like to thank you for reading this book. It has been an honor to share our stories and teachings with you. And remember, you are a very special person with a beautiful spiritual soul. You can and will connect through your soul to your power animal guide(s). Believe this and believe in yourself, believe in your dreams and aspirations. Through the assistance of your power animal guides and your own soul, you will and can enjoy your own unique spiritual journeys and find your spiritual pathway for your highest good.

Part Three:

Resources and References

Workshops, Individual Sessions, and Other Services

There is a companion CD to this book that introduces you to the heartbeats of the power animals and will assist you in practicing your shamanic journeys and meditations as described after each power animal story. You may order the CD by contacting me at the e-mail address listed below.

Do not hesitate to contact me if I can assist you in any way or if you would like to schedule a session or workshop with me. I would love to hear your power animal stories as well. Please visit my website at www.spirit-circle.com. I can be contacted at my e-mail address at frankistorlie@yahoo.com or by telephone at (509) 899-1324.

I offer the following workshops and individual sessions to everyone. The workshops can be offered in person if I am able to travel to your location, or they can be taken via the Internet. Individual sessions and psychic readings are offered in person, over the telephone, or via the Internet.

Medicine Wheel: I offer classes that share the teachings of the

Native American medicine wheel in relation to the each person, the earth, animals, trees, elements, and the environment. Participants will learn meditation practices that will assist them with achieving balance in their lives in a busy, chaotic world. Teachings will include traveling around the medicine wheel in relationship with the four seasons. Drumming and music are incorporated into the classes. Classes include working with rocks, crystals, power animals, and the elements. Participants will be taken on shamanic journeys. Participants will learn how to create sacred space using the medicine wheel.

Shamanic Journeys/Power Animals: Participants will learn how to travel shamanically and communicate with power animals and spirit guides. Participants will also learn meditation techniques and daily practices to empower themselves to go inward for information and answers, to hold higher vibratory levels. Participants also learn how to journey and merge with trees, rocks, power animals, and the elements.

Teachings of the Sacred Pyramids: This workshop will include meditations/journeys/healings within the sacred space of the pyramids and healings with the elements. Teachings include practices from the lineage of Isis and Mary Magdalene.

Individual Readings and Healings: I offer individual shamanic psychic readings and connecting with your power animals/totems. These sessions include energy healings with native drumming, crystals, chakra balancing, and soul healings/retrievals. These sessions will help each person to balance physically, mentally, emotionally, and spiritually to match their individual needs and goals.

House Blessings/Creating Sacred Space: I conduct house blessings for both newly constructed homes and older houses. I share how to create positive energy flow throughout the house and outdoor area surrounding the house. I share methods for creating sacred and safe space for home and family.

About the Author

Franki has been studying, practicing, and teaching spiritual classes and working individually with people for the past twenty years. Her background includes Native American ancestry. She has worked with and received training from other Native American shamans on various spiritual teachings. Franki specializes in practices of the sacred medicine wheel (not just Native American practices, but a broader span of teachings). She partners with nature to create safe and sacred space so that people can learn to meditate, connect to their inner self, connect to their power animal totem guides, and find balance in a very busy and chaotic world.

Franki's specialty is teaching and sharing with others the methods of shamanic journeying to help everyone to come in close communication and oneness with their soul. She provides personal readings for self-healing and connecting and communicating with each person's power animals, spirit guides, and nature. She shares how to start and continue a daily spiritual practice so that each person is healed and balanced physically, mentally, spiritually, and emotionally (body-mind-spirit balancing). She is a drummer and uses drumming in all her sessions and workshops.

Franki also offers chakra alignment and balancing, soul retrievals, emotional healing and releases, energy healings, crystal healings, native drumming healings, house and land blessings/clearings, and spiritual blessing ceremonies for the deceased.

Recommended Reading and Websites

Andrews, Ted. *Animal-Speak: The Spiritual and Magical Powers of Creatures Great and Small.* Woodbury, MN: Llewellyn Publications. 1994.

Websites:

www.spirit-circle.com

www.reflectingpond.com

www.thefamilyoflight.net